Little Buddies
PHONICS FUN

Bb Cc and Kk Dd Ff Gg Hh

Senior Editor: Janet D. Sweet
Design/Production: Alicia Triche
Art Director: Moonhee Pak
Managing Editor: Stacey Faulkner

The mini stories featured in this book originally appeared in the *Itty Bitty Phonics Readers* series,
© 2002 Creative Teaching Press (developed by Sue Lewis, written by Rozanne Lanczak Williams).

Table of Contents

Little Buddies Picture Clues & Phonics Fun Chart

Little Buddies like to have fun doing activities on their own—just like your own child—so look for these helpful picture clues in the activity directions.

 Write or trace or match

 Draw a circle around

 Cross out

 Say the name

 Color or draw a picture

 Cut out

 Glue

All six Little Buddies characters in this workbook—Bear, Coco, Daisy, Fox, Gus, and Henry—appear on collector's cards on the back side of the Little Buddies Phonics Fun Chart at the back of this book.

 Bb
 Cc
 Dd
 Ff
 Gg
 Hh

Look for the Little Buddies and their corresponding letter-sound pictures tucked into activities for each Little Buddies story. Have your child color, cut out, and glue the pictures to the inside of the chart to match with the characters on the back side. The Little Buddies Phonics Fun Chart can be used as a bookmark while your child enjoys the activities, or it can be cut apart to create personalized Little Buddies collector's cards—collect all 36 cards in the Little Buddies Phonics Fun series!

Phonics is one of the five essential steps that children must master in order to read. Practicing these five steps helps children learn to be good readers.

1 **Phonemic awareness.** This is the ability to recognize that spoken words are made up of many different individual sounds. For example, young learners need to hear the beginning, middle, and ending sounds when someone says *cat.*

2 **Phonics.** This is the ability to recognize that letters—and certain groups of letters—appearing in printed words represent different sounds. Children who have been taught phonics can accurately recognize familiar words automatically and can "decode," or figure out, new words.

3 **Reading fluency.** This is the ability to quickly and accurately decode a passage of words for meaning. Readers who are weak in fluency read slowly, word by word, focusing on decoding words instead of automatically recognizing them and understanding what they mean.

4 **Vocabulary development.** At this step, children actively build and expand their knowledge of the meanings and pronunciations of new words—both written and spoken.

5 **Reading comprehension.** This is the step when children become purposeful, active readers by acquiring strategies to understand, remember, and communicate what has been read.

Here are some tips for practicing phonics and promoting reading success at home.

- Talk with your child all the time about subjects that he or she finds interesting.

- Sing songs, recite rhymes and poems with repeating phrases, tell riddles and knock-knock jokes, and share stories that you enjoyed as a child.

- Make up stories while traveling in the car. Start with a silly beginning sentence, such as "Once upon a time, there was a skunk in our bathtub." Take turns adding new sentences aloud.

- Have your child describe a favorite story character, family relative, birthday present, or costume.

- Notice and talk about road signs, menus, and advertisements with your child when traveling. When at the grocery store, have your child read the letters and words on boxes and cans.

- Keep a wide variety of books, newspapers, and children's magazines at home, and carry reading material with you whenever you have free time, such as while waiting at the doctor's office. Let your child see you read often for your own benefit so your child realizes that reading is important and enjoyable.

- Establish a reading time, such as after dinner or before bed, to help your child get into the habit of reading every day. Make reading time a warm, pleasant experience. Sit close to your child, snuggle, laugh, and have fun. As you read aloud, ask your child about the pictures in the story, the characters, and what he or she thinks will happen next. Read aloud with expression. Use different voices for the different characters and add sound effects to the story.

- Visit the library often with your child. Take advantage of library story times, and pick out books together to bring home.

Each Little Buddy appears in a story that features the sound of a specific letter or cluster of letters. Meet the six Little Buddies and their featured letter sounds in this workbook:

Bear helps children learn the beginning sound of the letter **Bb**.

The letter **Bb** is Bear's favorite! It makes the sound that begins his name and the name of his favorite sport—baseball. Bear is curious and likes to explore things, especially the things inside his birthday boxes!

Coco helps children learn the beginning sound of the letters **Cc** and **Kk**.

When Coco can't sleep, she snuggles under her covers and counts her favorite things, like candy, cakes, and kittens. Look for Coco in Little Buddies Phonics Fun Book 6, also.

Daisy helps children learn the beginning sound of the letter **Dd**.

Daisy definitely likes to dance! She can sometimes be a bit dramatic, but it's never dull when this delightful duck dances! Look for Daisy in Little Buddies Phonics Fun Book 3, also.

Fox helps children learn the beginning sound of the letter **Ff**.

Fox likes to roller skate. It's one of his favorite sports because it makes him fast on his feet. It's fun to watch Fox figure out fancy footwork. When he gets going too fast, though, his friends think he's funny.

Gus helps children learn the beginning sound of the letter **Gg**.

Gus likes to spend time with his friends and family. It's hard for him to say good-bye unless he's going to Grandma's house. Look for Gus in Little Buddies Phonics Fun Book 6, also.

Henry helps children learn the beginning sound of the letter **Hh**.

Henry is a happy-go-lucky hippo who is never in a hurry—except when he is hungry. Whenever his dad cooks hot dogs and hamburgers, Henry happily hurries home!

Little Buddies Phonics Fun
Story Words

Each Little Buddies Phonics Fun story features words that target a specific beginning letter sound. Parents, prior to reading each story, you may want to read these words aloud with your child. Emphasizing beginning sounds and their corresponding letters helps support your child's mastery of phonics, a critical early step in achieving reading success.

The story **What Is in Bear's Box?** features these words that begin with the sound of the letter **Bb**:

- Bear's
- box
- ball
- bat
- buttons
- bugs
- but
- big
- balloon
- bye-bye
- Bear

The story **Coco Can Count** features these words that begin with the sound of the letters **Cc/Kk**:

- count
- candy
- cakes
- cookies
- can
- cats
- kittens
- cows
- kings
- keys
- kids
- kites

The story **Daisy Dances** features these words that begin with the sound of the letter **Dd**:

- Daisy
- dance
- dogs
- ducks
- dinosaurs
- do

The story **What Is Funny?** features these words that begin with the sound of the letter **Ff**:

- funny
- face
- fast
- fox
- fat
- fish
- five
- fingers
- four
- feet
- farmers

The story **Good-bye, Gus!** features these words that begin with the sound of the letter **Gg**:

- Good-bye
- goldfish
- goose
- gorilla
- garage
- garden
- gate
- guess
- going
- Grandma's

The story **Hurry Up, Henry** features these words that begin with the sound of the letter **Hh**:

- hurry
- Henry
- Hen
- Hog
- Hippo
- Hare
- hungry
- hurray
- hot dogs
- hamburgers
- hundreds

What Is in Bear's Box?

 Trace the letter **Bb**.

These things begin with the sound of **b**.

 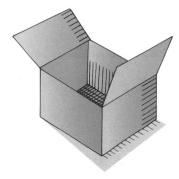 

 Color the balloon.

 Cut out the balloon.

 Glue it on the **Bb** space inside the Little Buddies Phonics Chart.

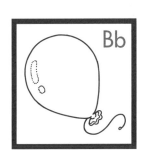

Bb

○ Circle each letter **b**.

b   d   b   p

p   b   d   b

○ Circle each letter **B**.

B   P   F   B

R   B   B   R

○ Circle the things that begin with the sound of **b**.

8

What is in Bear's box?

 Trace the letter **B** in .

 Trace the letter **b** in .

A ball!

Color the picture that begins with the sound of **b**.

Little Buddies Phonics Fun • Book 1 • Gr. PreK–K © 2012 Creative Teaching Press

What is in Bear's box?
A bat!

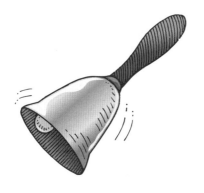 Circle the things that begin with the sound of **b**.

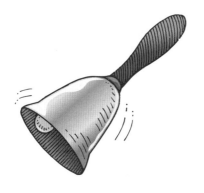

What is in Bear's box?
Buttons!

Circle the things that begin with the sound of **b**.

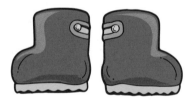

Little Buddies Phonics Fun • Book 1 • Gr. PreK–K © 2012 Creative Teaching Press

What is in Bear's box?
Bugs!

 Cross out the things that do **not** begin with the sound of **b**.

But what is in Bear's big box?

Draw pictures of 2 things that begin with the sound of **b**.

Little Buddies Phonics Fun • Book 1 • Gr. PreK–K © 2012 Creative Teaching Press

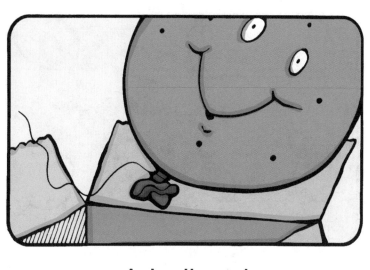

A balloon!

 Match the pictures to their story words.

 • • bear

 • • box

 • • balloon

Bye-bye, Bear!

 Write the missing letter.

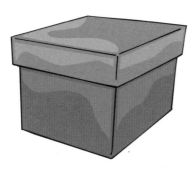

___ ox

___ ear

Little Buddies Phonics Fun • Book 1 • Gr. PreK–K © 2012 Creative Teaching Press

"Before Bed" Mini Book

Mini Book Directions: Tear out pages 17–20. Cut the pages apart along the solid lines. Arrange the pages together in order. Staple the pages to make a little book that begins with **Before Bed**. Enjoy your book!

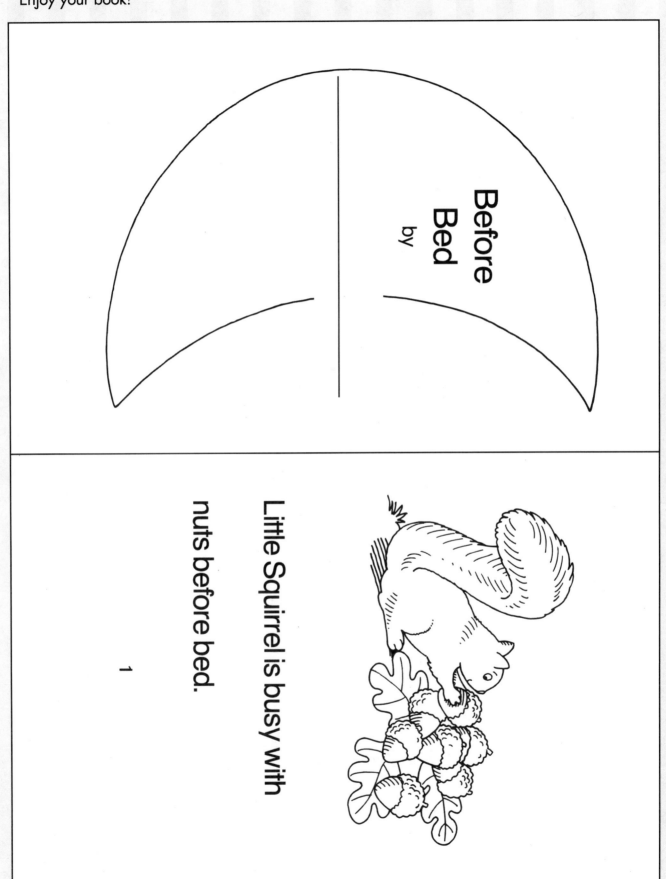

Before
Bed

by

Little Squirrel is busy with

nuts before bed.

1

Little Buddies Phonics Fun • Book 1 • Gr. PreK–K © 2012 Creative Teaching Press

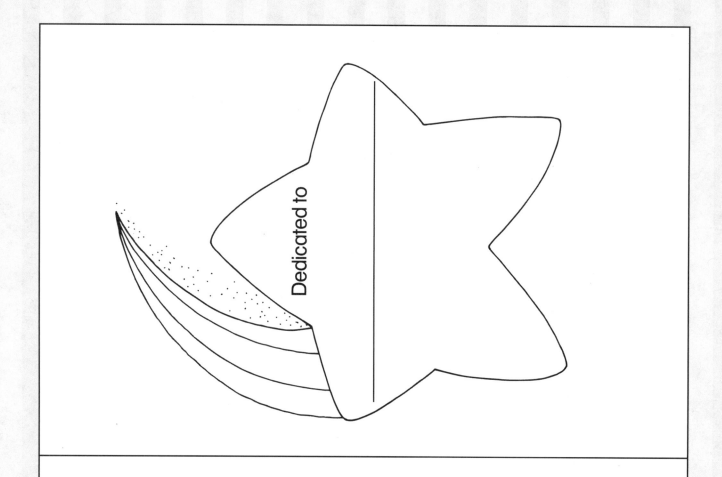

Dedicated to

Little Bear is busy with

berries before bed.

2

Little Bunny is busy with

carrots before bed.

5

Little Bee is busy with

pollen before bed.

3

Little Buddies are busy with

toys before bed.

The End

6

Little Beaver is busy with

logs before bed.

4

Coco Can Count

 Trace the letter **Cc** and the letter **Kk**.

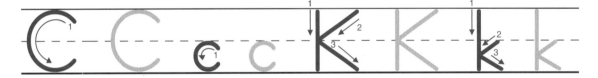

These things begin with the sound of **c/k**.

 Color the cake.

 Cut out the cake.

 Glue it on the **Cc/Kk** space inside the Little Buddies Phonics Chart.

Cc/Kk

Cc/Kk

Circle each letter c and k.

c   b   k   d

k   c   b   f

Circle each letter C and K.

K   S   C   C

B   C   K   D

Circle the things that begin with the sound of c/k.

 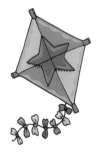 

Little Buddies Phonics Fun • Book 1 • Gr. PreK–K © 2012 Creative Teaching Press

Count the candy.

 Trace the letter **C** in  Coco .

 Trace the letter **k** in  kite .

Count the cakes.

Circle the things that begin with the sound of **c/k**.

Little Buddies Phonics Fun • Book 1 • Gr. PreK–K © 2012 Creative Teaching Press

Count the cookies
we can make.

 Color the picture that begins with the sound of **c/k**.

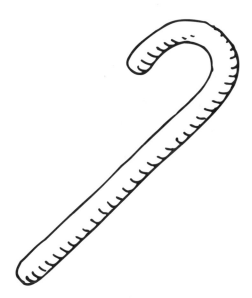

Count the cats,
and kittens, too.

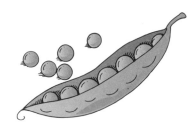 Cross out the things that do **not** begin with the sound of **c/k**.

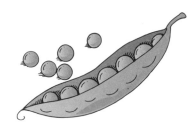

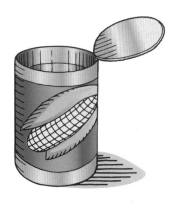

Count the cows that go, "Moo, moo."

 Match the pictures to their story words.

 •　　　• cat

 •　　　• cow

 •　　　• candy

Count the kings.

 Draw pictures of 2 things that begin with the sound of **c/k**.

Count the keys.

 Cross out the words that do **not** begin with the letter **c** or **k**.

candle   key   boy

hand   cap   camel

cup   carrot   and

Count the kids
and kites you see.

 Say the name of each picture.

 Match the beginning sound of each picture to its letter.

 • • c/k • •

 • • b • •

"Cookies, Please!" Mini Book

Mini Book Directions: Tear out pages 31–34. Cut the pages apart along the solid lines. Arrange the pages together in order. Staple the pages to make a little book that begins with **Cookies, Please**. Enjoy your book!

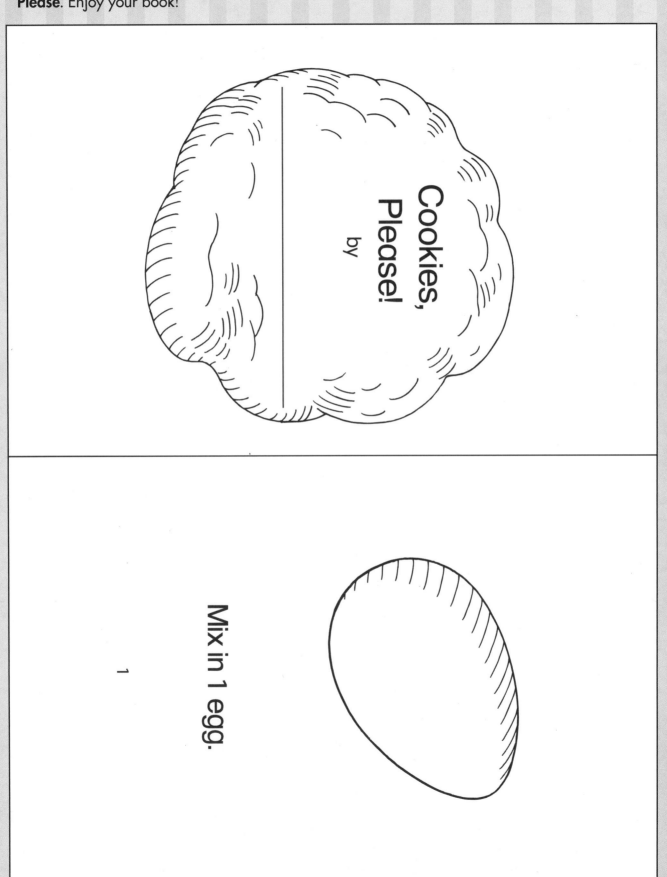

Cookies,
Please!

by

Mix in 1 egg.

1

Dedicated to

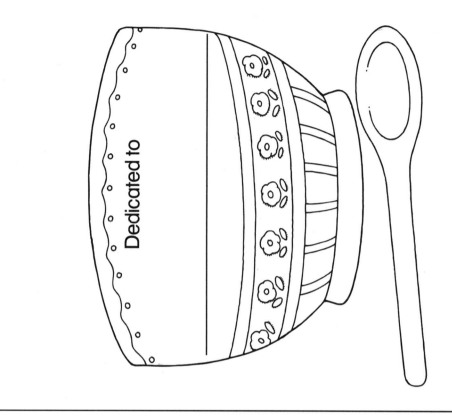

Mix in 2 cups of sugar.

2

Mix in 5 scoops of nuts.

5

Mix in 3 cups of flour.

3

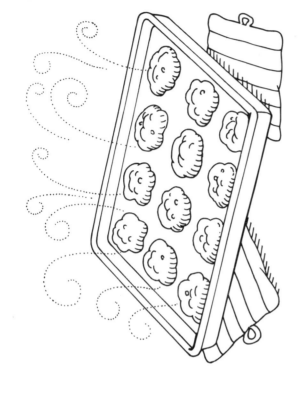

Bake, bake, bake.

Cookies, please!

The End

6

Mix in 4 scoops of chocolate.

4

Daisy Dances

 Trace the letter **Dd**.

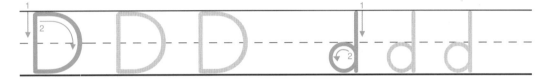

These things begin with the sound of **d**.

 Color the dog.

 Cut out the dog.

 Glue it on the **Dd** space inside the Little Buddies Phonics Chart.

Dd

Circle each letter d.

d	d	b	h
h	d	d	b

Circle each letter D.

D	O	D	D
B	D	D	C

Circle the things that begin with the sound of d.

Little Buddies Phonics Fun • Book 1 • Gr. PreK–K © 2012 Creative Teaching Press

Daisy likes to dance.

 Trace the letter **D** in .

 Trace the letter **d** in .

Little Buddies Phonics Fun • Book 1 • Gr. PreK–K © 2012 Creative Teaching Press

Dogs like to dance, too.

 Color the picture that begins with the sound of **d**.

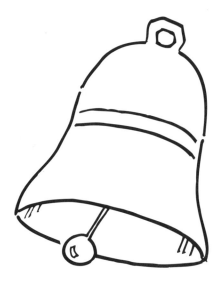

Little Buddies Phonics Fun • Book 1 • Gr. PreK–K © 2012 Creative Teaching Press

Daisy likes to dance.

 Circle the things that begin with the sound of **d**.

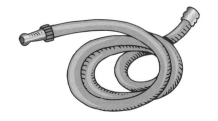

Ducks like to dance, too.

 Match the pictures to their story words.

 • • **Daisy**

 • • **duck**

 • • **dog**

Little Buddies Phonics Fun • Book 1 • Gr. PreK–K © 2012 Creative Teaching Press

Daisy likes to dance.

 Cross out the things that do **not** begin with the sound of **d**.

Dinosaurs like to dance, too.

 Say the name of each picture.

 Match the beginning sound of each picture to its letter.

   •   • **Dd** •   •

   •   • **b** •   •

Little Buddies Phonics Fun • Book 1 • Gr. PreK–K © 2012 Creative Teaching Press

Dance with Daisy!

 Cross out the words that do **not** begin with the letter **d**.

dance	box	like
done	day	be
do	kite	crunch

Do the Daisy Dance!

 Cut out the letters in the boxes below.

 Glue each letter(s) next to a picture that begins with that letter sound.

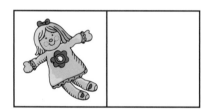

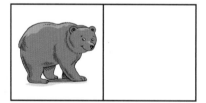

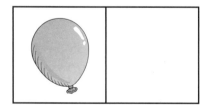

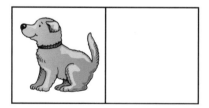

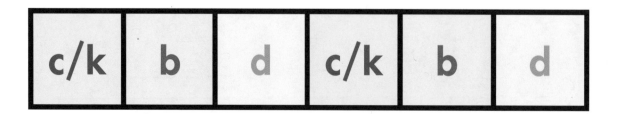

c/k   b   d   c/k   b   d

Little Buddies Phonics Fun • Book 1 • Gr. PreK–K © 2012 Creative Teaching Press

"Day and Night" Mini Book

Mini Book Directions: Tear out pages 45–48. Cut the pages apart along the solid lines. Arrange the pages together in order. Staple the pages to make a little book that begins with **Day and Night**. Enjoy your book!

Day and Night
by

An owl is awake all night.

It sleeps all day.

1

Little Buddies Phonics Fun • Book 1 • Gr. PreK–K © 2012 Creative Teaching Press

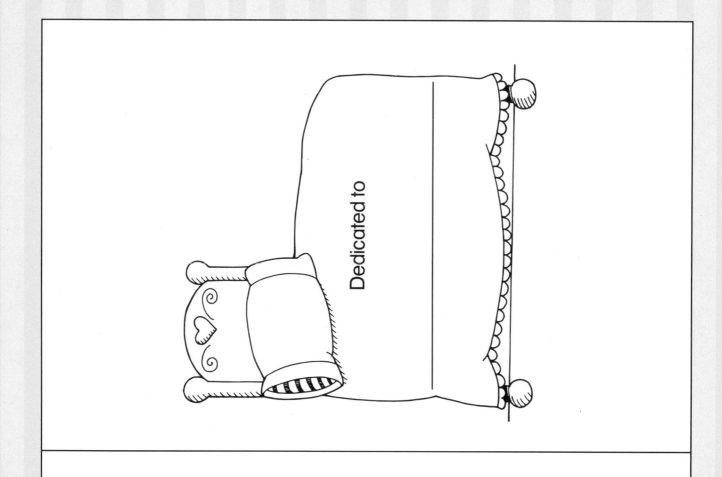

Dedicated to

A ladybug is awake all day.

It sleeps all night.

2

A cricket is awake all night.

It sleeps all day.

5

A bat is awake all night.

It sleeps all day.

3

Little Buddies Phonics Fun • Book 1 • Gr. PreK–K © 2012 Creative Teaching Press

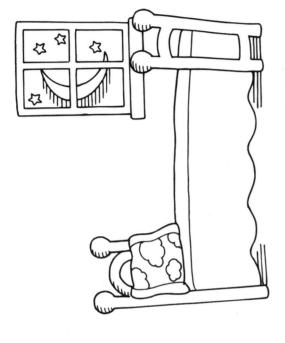

I am awake all day.

I sleep all night.

The End

6

A squirrel is awake all day.

It sleeps all night.

4

Little Buddies Phonics Fun • Book 1 • Gr. PreK–K © 2012 Creative Teaching Press

What Is Funny?

 Trace the letter **Ff**.

These things begin with the sound of **f**.

 Color the fish.

 Cut out the fish.

 Glue it on the **Ff** space inside the Little Buddies Phonics Chart.

Circle each letter **f**.

k   f   b   p

f   t   f   t

Circle each letter **F**.

F   B   F   B

F   F   D   B

Circle the things that begin with the sound of **f**.

Little Buddies Phonics Fun • Book 1 • Gr. PreK–K © 2012 Creative Teaching Press

What is funny? A funny face.

 Trace the letter F in Fox.

 Trace the letter f in fish.

Little Buddies Phonics Fun • Book 1 • Gr. PreK–K © 2012 Creative Teaching Press

A fast, funny fox.

Circle the things that begin with the sound of **f**.

Little Buddies Phonics Fun • Book 1 • Gr. PreK–K © 2012 Creative Teaching Press

A fat, funny fish.

 Color the picture that begins with the sound of f.

A funny little box.

Cross out the things that do **not** begin with the sound of **f**.

Five funny fingers.

 Draw pictures of 2 things that begin with the sound of f.

Four funny feet.

 Match the pictures to their story words.

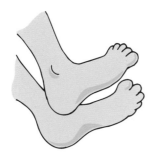 •   • **fish**

 •   • **fingers**

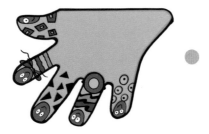 •   • **feet**

Little Buddies Phonics Fun • Book 1 • Gr. PreK–K © 2012 Creative Teaching Press

Five funny farmers.

 Cross out the words that do **not** begin with the letter **f**.

funny	face	box
little	five	fat
fast	fingers	sheep

Little Buddies Phonics Fun • Book 1 • Gr. PreK–K © 2012 Creative Teaching Press

And four funny sheep!

 Write the missing letter.

4 ____our

 ____armers

Little Buddies Phonics Fun • Book 1 • Gr. PreK–K © 2012 Creative Teaching Press

"Family" Mini Book

Mini Book Directions: Tear out pages 59–62. Cut the pages apart along the solid lines. Arrange the pages together in order. Staple the pages to make a little book that begins with **Family**. Enjoy your book!

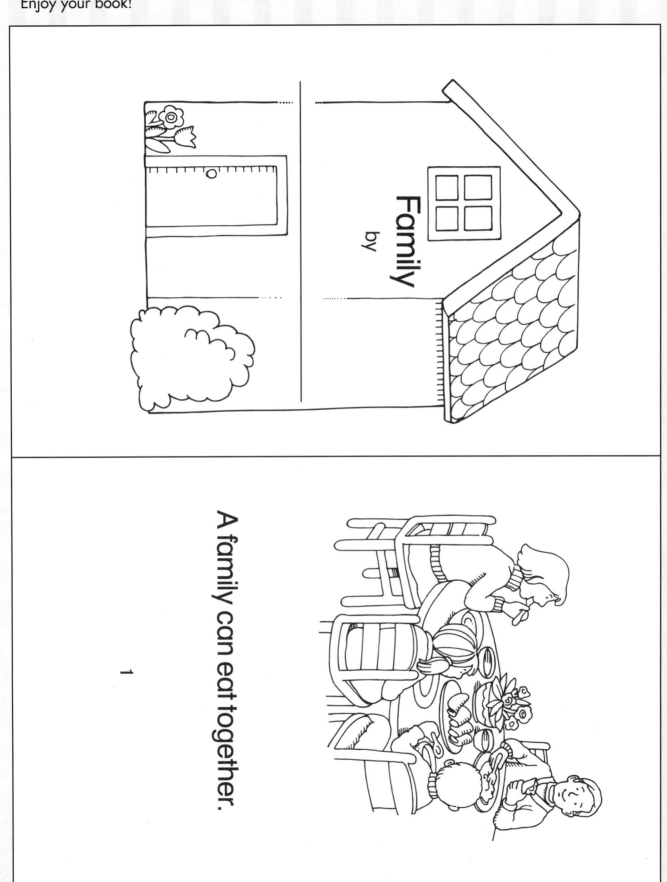

Family
by

A family can eat together.

1

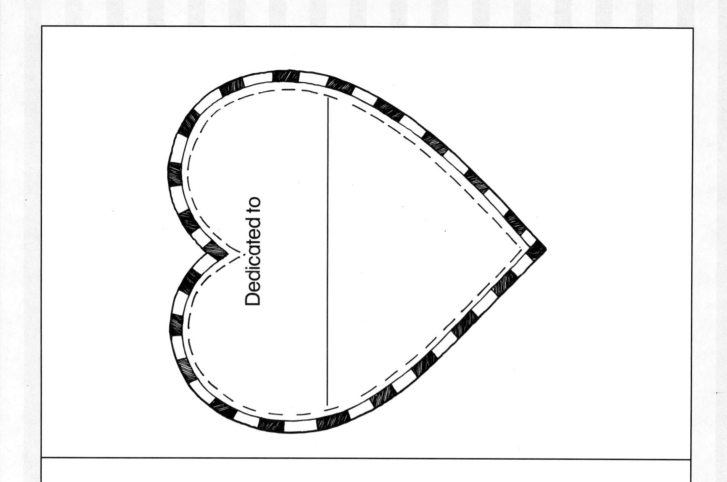

Dedicated to

A family can walk together.

2

Little Buddies Phonics Fun • Book 1 • Gr. PreK–K © 2012 Creative Teaching Press

A family can have fun
together.

5

A family can see friends
together.

3

Little Buddies Phonics Fun • Book 1 • Gr. PreK–K © 2012 Creative Teaching Press

Who is in your family?

The End

6

A family can exercise

together.

4

Good-bye, Gus!

 Trace the letter **Gg**.

These things begin with the sound of **g**.

 Color the goat.

 Cut out the goat.

 Glue it on the **Gg** space inside the Little Buddies Phonics Chart.

Little Buddies Phonics Fun • Book 1 • Gr. PreK–K © 2012 Creative Teaching Press

Gg

Circle each letter g.

g	g	p	j
y	g	j	y

Circle each letter G.

B	G	G	D
G	D	G	J

Circle the things that begin with the sound of g.

Good-bye, goldfish!

 Trace the letter **G** in Gus.

 Trace the letter **g** in goldfish.

Little Buddies Phonics Fun • Book 1 • Gr. PreK–K © 2012 Creative Teaching Press

Good-bye, goose!

Color the picture that begins with the sound of g.

Good-bye, gorilla!

 Circle the things that begin with the sound of **g**.

Good-bye, garage!

 Match the pictures to their story words.

 • • **goose**

 • • **gorilla**

 • • **goldfish**

Good-bye, garden!

 Cross out the things that do **not** begin with the sound of **g**.

Good-bye, gate!

 Say the name of each picture.

 Match the beginning sound of each picture to its letter.

 • • Ff • •

 • • Gg • •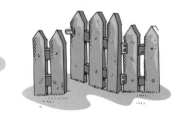

Little Buddies Phonics Fun • Book 1 • Gr. PreK–K © 2012 Creative Teaching Press

Guess where I am going.

○ Circle the words that begin with the letter **g**.

garage   gate   me

house   gum   but

going   good-bye   where

I am going
to Grandma's house!

 Write the missing letter.

 __orilla

__arden

"Go Up!" Mini Book

Mini Book Directions: Tear out pages 73–76. Cut the pages apart along the solid lines. Arrange the pages together in order. Staple the pages to make a little book that begins with **"Go Up!"** Enjoy your book!

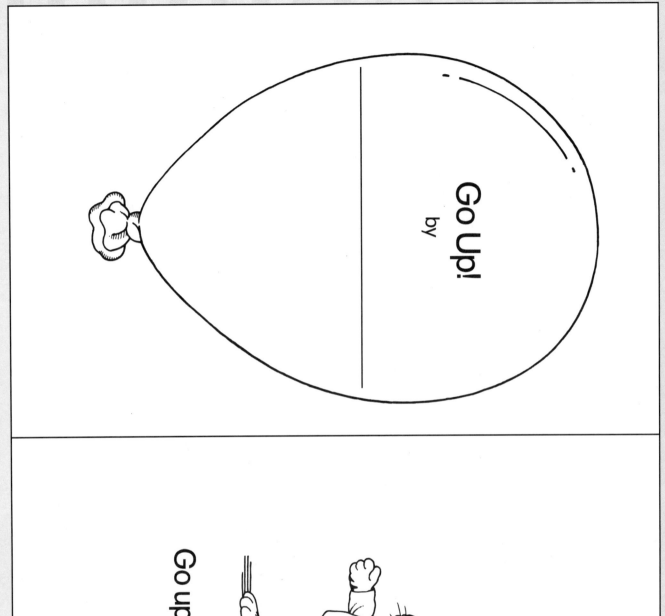

Go Up!
by

Go up, red balloon!

1

Little Buddies Phonics Fun • Book 1 • Gr. PreK–K © 2012 Creative Teaching Press

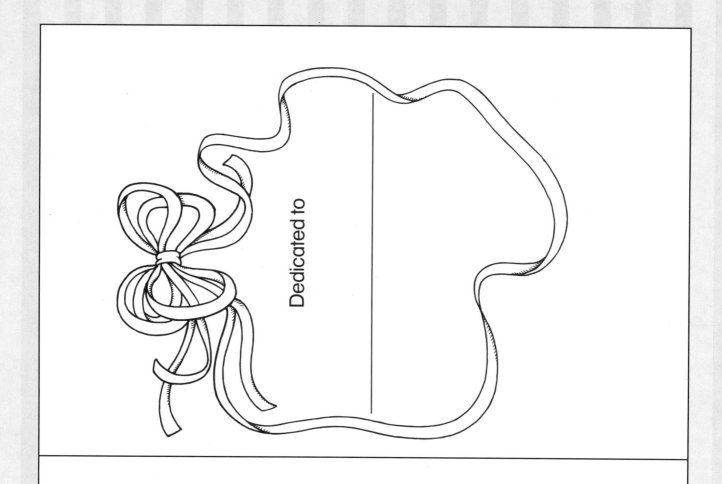

Dedicated to

_____

Go up, yellow balloon!

2

Little Buddies Phonics Fun • Book 1 • Gr. PreK–K © 2012 Creative Teaching Press

Go up, orange balloon!

5

Go up, green balloon!

3

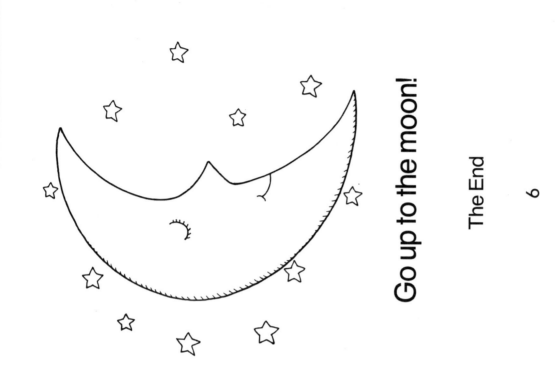

Go up to the moon!

The End

6

Go up, blue balloon!

4

Little Buddies Phonics Fun • Book 1 • Gr. PreK–K © 2012 Creative Teaching Press

Hurry up, Henry!

 Trace the letter **Hh**.

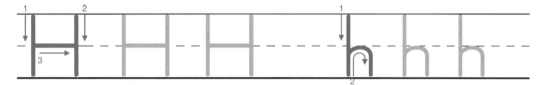

These things begin with the sound of **h**.

 Color the horse.

 Cut out the horse.

 Glue it on the **Hh** space inside the Little Buddies Phonics Chart.

Circle each letter **h**.

h	b	h	d
b	h	d	h

Circle each letter **H**.

H	B	H	B
F	H	H	F

Circle the things that begin with the sound of **h**.

"Hurry up, Henry," said Hen.

 Trace the letter **H** in .

 Trace the letter **h** in .

Little Buddies Phonics Fun • Book 1 • Gr. PreK–K © 2012 Creative Teaching Press

"Hurry up, Henry,"
said Hog.

Circle the things that begin with the sound of **h**.

"Hurry up, Henry,"
said Hippo.

 Color the picture that begins with the sound of **h**.

"Hurry up, Henry," said Hare.

Cross out the things that do **not** begin with the sound of **h**.

"We're hungry!"

 Draw pictures of 2 things that begin with the sound of **h**.

"Hurray!" said Henry.

🗨 Say the name of each picture.

✏ Match the beginning sound of each picture to its letter.

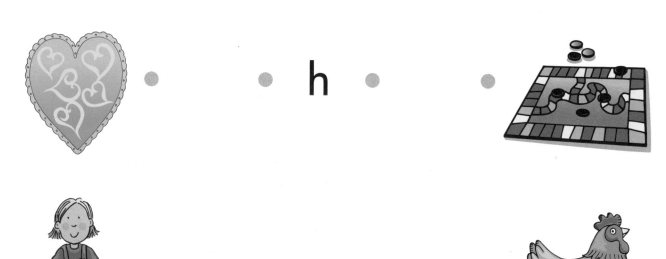

h

g

"Hot dogs and hamburgers!"

 Cross out the words that do **not** begin with the letter **h**.

hurray   pig   hare

hurry   hot   said

dinner   dad   hungry

"Hundreds of hot dogs
and hamburgers!"

 Cut out the letters in the boxes below.

 Glue each letter(s) next to a picture that begins with that letter sound.

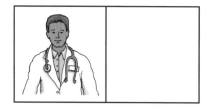

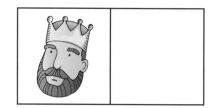

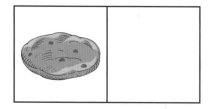

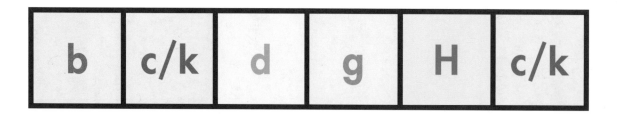

| b | c/k | d | g | H | c/k |

Little Buddies Phonics Fun • Book 1 • Gr. PreK–K © 2012 Creative Teaching Press

"Halloween Party" Mini Book

Mini Book Directions: Tear out pages 87–90. Cut the pages apart along the solid lines. Arrange the pages together in order. Staple the pages to make a little book that begins with **Halloween Party**. Enjoy your book!

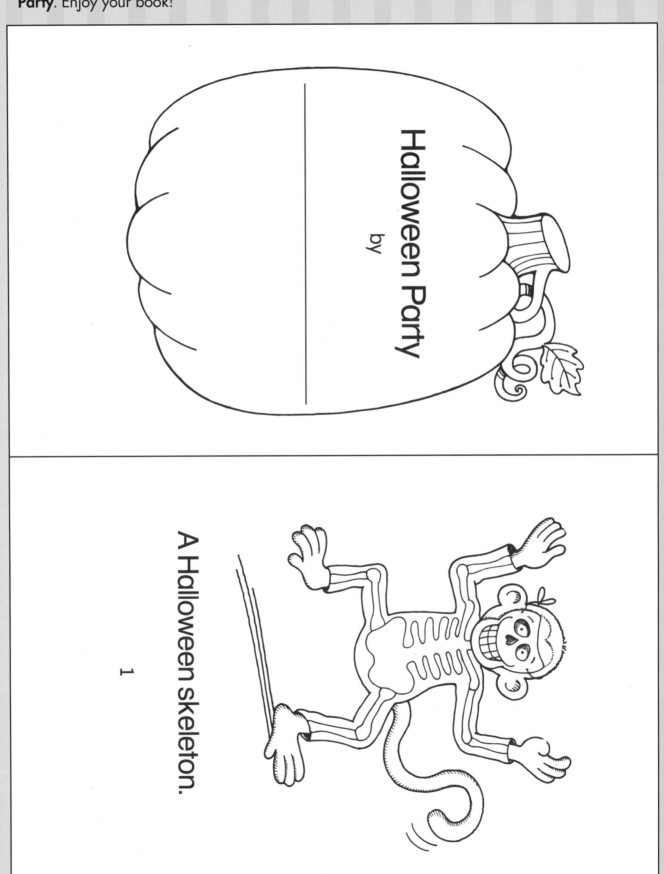

Halloween Party

by

A Halloween skeleton.

1

Little Buddies Phonics Fun • Book 1 • Gr. PreK–K © 2012 Creative Teaching Press

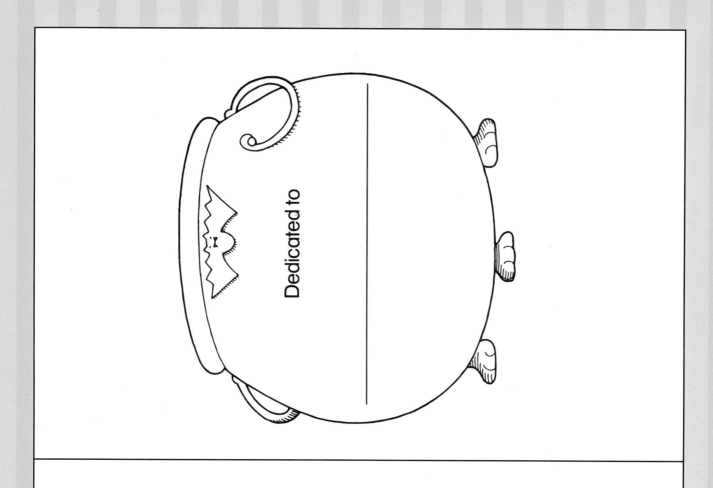

Dedicated to

_____

A Halloween bat.

2

Little Buddies Phonics Fun • Book 1 • Gr. PreK–K © 2012 Creative Teaching Press

A Halloween ghost.

5

A Halloween monster.

3

What do you like the most?

The End

6

A Halloween cat.

4

Little Buddies Phonics Fun • Book 1 • Gr. PreK–K © 2012 Creative Teaching Press

Answer Key

PAGE 8

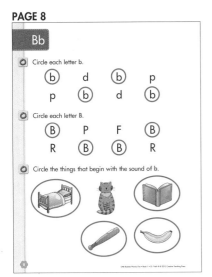

Bb

Circle each letter b.

b d b p
p b d b

Circle each letter B.

B P F B
R B B R

Circle the things that begin with the sound of b.

PAGE 10

baseball

PAGE 11

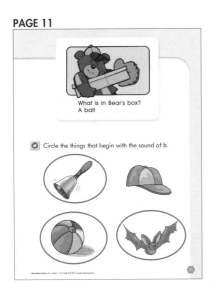

What is in Bear's box?
A bat!

Circle the things that begin with the sound of b.

PAGE 12

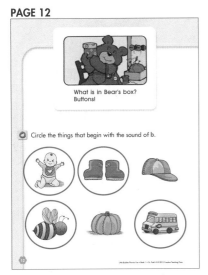

What is in Bear's box?
Buttons!

Circle the things that begin with the sound of b.

PAGE 13

What is in Bear's box?
Bugs!

Cross out the things that do not begin with the sound of b.

PAGE 15

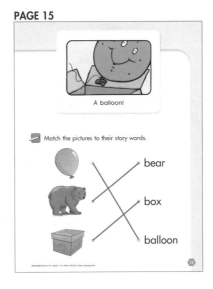

A balloon!

Match the pictures to their story words.

bear

box

balloon

PAGE 16

box
Bear

PAGE 22

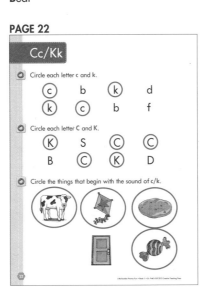

Cc/Kk

Circle each letter c and k.

c b k d
k c b f

Circle each letter C and K.

K S C C
B C K D

Circle the things that begin with the sound of c/k.

PAGE 24

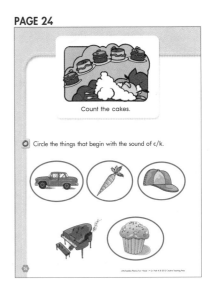

Count the cakes.

Circle the things that begin with the sound of c/k.

PAGE 25

cane

PAGE 26

Count the cats,
and kittens, too.

Cross out the things that do not begin with the sound of c/k.

PAGE 27

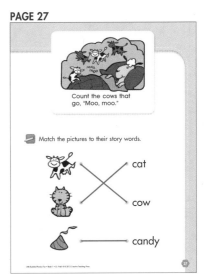

Count the cows that
go, "Moo, moo."

Match the pictures to their story words.

cat

cow

candy

PAGE 29

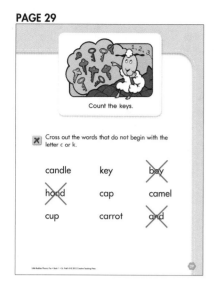

Count the keys.

☒ Cross out the words that do not begin with the letter c or k.

candle　　key　　~~boy~~

~~hand~~　　cap　　camel

cup　　carrot　　~~and~~

PAGE 39

Daisy likes to dance.

◯ Circle the things that begin with the sound of d.

PAGE 42

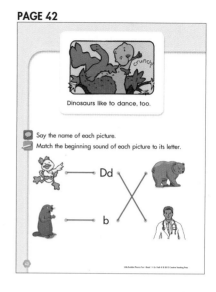

Dinosaurs like to dance, too.

Say the name of each picture.

Match the beginning sound of each picture to its letter.

Dd

b

PAGE 30

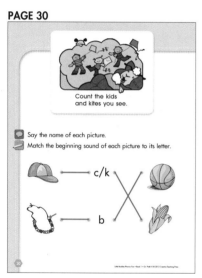

Count the kids and kites you see.

Say the name of each picture.

Match the beginning sound of each picture to its letter.

c/k

b

PAGE 40

Ducks like to dance, too.

Match the pictures to their story words.

Daisy

duck

dog

PAGE 43

Dance with Daisy!

☒ Cross out the words that do not begin with the letter d.

dance　　~~box~~　　~~like~~

done　　day　　~~be~~

do　　~~kite~~　　crunch

PAGE 36

Dd

◯ Circle each letter d.

(d)　(d)　b　h

h　(d)　(d)　b

◯ Circle each letter D.

(D)　O　(D)　(D)

B　(D)　(D)　C

◯ Circle the things that begin with the sound of d.

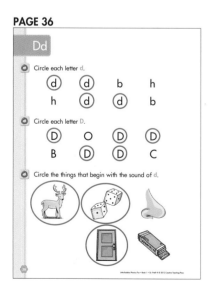

PAGE 41

Daisy likes to dance.

☒ Cross out the things that do not begin with the sound of d.

PAGE 44

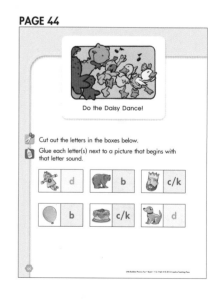

Do the Daisy Dance!

Cut out the letters in the boxes below.

Glue each letter(s) next to a picture that begins with that letter sound.

d	b	c/k
b	c/k	d

PAGE 38

desk

PAGE 50

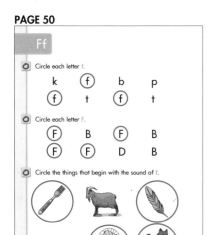

PAGE 52

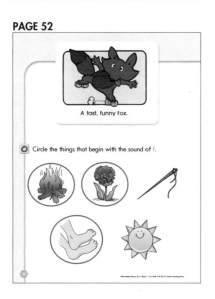

PAGE 53
fire

PAGE 54

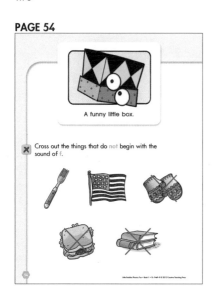

PAGE 56

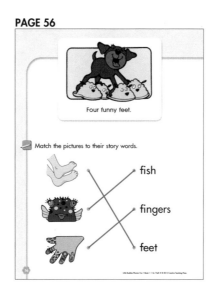

PAGE 57

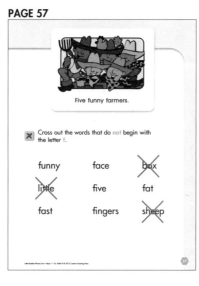

PAGE 58
four
farmers

PAGE 64

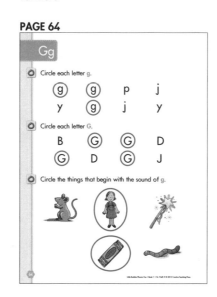

PAGE 66
gorilla

PAGE 67

PAGE 68

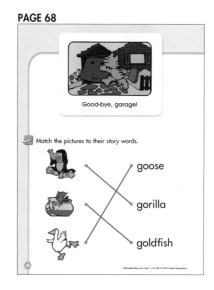

PAGE 69

PAGE 70

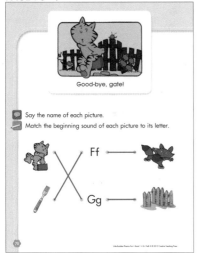

Good-bye, gate!

Say the name of each picture.
Match the beginning sound of each picture to its letter.

Ff

Gg

PAGE 71

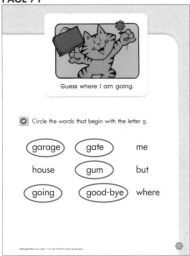

Guess where I am going.

Circle the words that begin with the letter g.

(garage)   (gate)   me

house   (gum)   but

(going)   (good-bye)   where

PAGE 72
gorilla
garden

PAGE 78

Hh

Circle each letter h.

(h)   b   (h)   d
b   (h)   d   (h)

Circle each letter H.

(H)   B   (H)   B
F   (H)   (H)   F

Circle the things that begin with the sound of h.

PAGE 80

"Hurry up, Henry,"
said Hog.

Circle the things that begin with the sound of h.

PAGE 81
hamburger

PAGE 82

"Hurry up, Henry," said Hare.

Cross out the things that do not begin with the sound of h.

PAGE 84

"Hurray!" said Henry.

Say the name of each picture.
Match the beginning sound of each picture to its letter.

h

g

PAGE 85

"Hot dogs and hamburgers!"

Cross out the words that do not begin with the letter h.

hurray   ~~pig~~   hare

hurry   hot   ~~said~~

~~dinner~~   ~~dad~~   hungry

PAGE 86

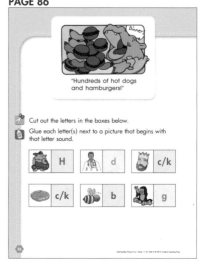

"Hundreds of hot dogs
and hamburgers!"

Cut out the letters in the boxes below.
Glue each letter(s) next to a picture that begins with that letter sound.

	H		d		c/k
	c/k		b		g

PHONICS

FUNtastic Job!

Book 1: Bb Cc/Kk Dd Ff Gg Hh

_____

Signed

_____

Name

_____

Date